Press Work for Women: A Text Book for the Young Woman Journalist. What to Write, How to Write It, and Where to Send It

Frances H. Low

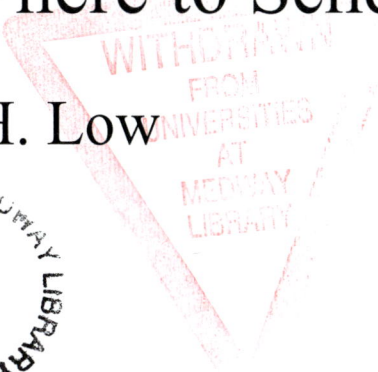

Nabu Public Domain Reprints:

You are holding a reproduction of an original work published before 1923 that is in the public domain in the United States of America, and possibly other countries. You may freely copy and distribute this work as no entity (individual or corporate) has a copyright on the body of the work. This book may contain prior copyright references, and library stamps (as most of these works were scanned from library copies). These have been scanned and retained as part of the historical artifact.

This book may have occasional imperfections such as missing or blurred pages, poor pictures, errant marks, etc. that were either part of the original artifact, or were introduced by the scanning process. We believe this work is culturally important, and despite the imperfections, have elected to bring it back into print as part of our continuing commitment to the preservation of printed works worldwide. We appreciate your understanding of the imperfections in the preservation process, and hope you enjoy this valuable book.

PRESS WORK for WOMEN.

Proof :—

France—where so much has been done in recent times to advance a knowledge of the merits of the old Cremonese makers, and especialy as she has produced (partly as a result of of her researches) the greatest violinmaker that has lived since Joseph del Jesu died—well might have claimed the place of honour after Italy.

Early references to the violin seem to be as scarce in the literature of france as they are in that of any other country, it is chiefly from accounts and paintings of fêtes that any knowledge concerng its history. There is a picture painted about 1845 caled the "Psaultier du roi René," containing a figure playing upon a viol which approaches the violin in shape, having a circular sound hole in the centre. This René fought in Italy in 1842 in conjunction with the Venetians, against the Duke of Ferrara, as he was a great patron of the fine arts, it is supposed that he bought this instrument or its design from the later country.

There can be divined

Press Work for Women.

A Text Book for the Young Woman Journalist.

What to Write,
How to Write It, and
Where to Send It.

By

FRANCES H. LOW.

Author of "Queen Victoria's Dolls," "The Little Men in Scarlet," &c.

LONDON:
L. UPCOTT GILL, BAZAAR BUILDINGS, DRURY LANE, W.C.
NEW YORK:
CHARLES SCRIBNER'S SONS, 153-157, FIFTH AVENUE.
1904.

LONDON:
L. UPCOTT GILL, LONDON AND COUNTY PRINTING WORKS,
BAZAAR BUILDINGS, W.C.

CONTENTS.

PRESS WORK FOR WOMEN.

PART I.

PRELIMINARY REMARKS.

THE occupation of journalism is daily becoming more attractive to the average fairly well-educated woman. This is not surprising when we compare its comparatively easy conditions of success of a modest kind with the prolonged training, the accumulated knowledge, and high standard of qualification needed, for instance, by the woman teacher to-day. The great majority of teachers have gone through college training, the cost of which is rarely less than £400 to £500 (1920 to 2400 dolls.), and have gained degrees, in many cases even honours degrees, and yet their earnings are generally less than the average earnings of the journalist who has had no training at all, and in many successful instances has no mental qualifications which in any other occupation would be estimated at a high rate. Moreover, under the

B

present dispensation of journalistic things, it is quite possible for the novice in journalism to make a small income from the start, a situation that exists in no other form of employment open to women; for even in the higher branches of domestic service the worker is presumed to know her trade before she demands remuneration for her services.

It is in no way difficult, then, to account for the immense popularity of journalism. It is infinitely more difficult to give wise counsel upon the two or three important points that must enter into the consideration of the genuine bread-winner: and it is to this type of woman, as distinguished from the well-to-do person, unfortunately too prevalent to-day—seeing how unfair is her competition with the legitimate wage-earner—that I am addressing myself. She may be expected to take up journalism seriously as her sisters take up teaching or nursing.

Now, the first point for consideration is, how far the vocation is suited to a well-educated intelligent woman. Is the work in itself worth doing? Does it offer opportunities for mental advancement and development? I think a considerable amount of disappointment and failure will be saved if I state boldly, as a result of fifteen years' practical experience, that women's journalism, as conducted at present (and in this I include every department of journalism open to women), is not worthy of the powers, knowledge, and training of the *highly cultivated* woman; that, in fact, it is my honest conviction, which I could support by unanswerable proof if need be, that there is absolutely no scope in the modern newspaper world for talent of a delicate order. Twenty years ago it was not so, and the cultivated woman having a light, graceful style, delicate fancy, and charm of handling which "touches nothing that it does not adorn," and having, above all, an essentially feminine attitude towards life—the complement of the rougher, robuster masculine attitude—could easily and profitably dispose of her work in the best journals read by men and women.

In a brief introduction of this kind I am not able to dwell upon this point, but I must emphasise my unshakable conviction that unless there be a complete revolution in women's journalism, the most delicate literary talent of brilliant writers, such as Madame de Girardin, exhibited in her matchless "Lettres Parisiennes" —pure journalism in every sense of the word, yet journalism raised to a fine art—will be wholly superfluous. Moreover, I seriously advise any cultivated woman determined to do only the finer kind of journalistic work to choose some other mode of bread-winning, if she would not find herself in middle age doomed to hack work and a poverty very close to destitution.

On the other hand, for a woman moderately intelligent, having the ordinary High School education and the ordinary ideals and ambitions of the average woman, it must be admitted that there is much to be said in favour of journalism as a means of earning a fair livelihood.

This brings me to the second salient point for consideration in this connection. Does journalism offer the possibility of earning a fair and regular income, which will allow of decent maintenance and saving for old age and sickness?

To lay down the law on this point, or even to give exact data, would be most imprudent; for out of the hundreds of women calling themselves journalists and belonging to journalistic clubs and societies, only a small proportion wholly maintain themselves by their earnings; and the statements that from time to time appear in the Press as to the elegant dress of this well-known journalist, or the expensive entertainments given by another, must not be taken as affording any clue to the incomes actually earned by these individuals. In nine cases out of ten, such ladies have well-to-do husbands or fathers, who contribute to their support; and an income which would barely suffice to keep a real bread-winner in food and clothes makes a very handsome pocket-money allowance for pleasures, dress, &c.

Speaking from my own actual experience, and that of a tolerably wide circle of other *bonâ-fide* journalists, coupled with careful enquiries and investigations extending over the last ten years that enable me to speak with a fair degree of certainty upon this point, I am convinced that the majority of competent journalists cannot reckon upon a larger income from their own earnings than £100 to £150 (480 to 720 dolls.) a year.

A considerable number of women journalists work in their "copy" with the advertisement department, and their earnings are undoubtedly higher, in some cases reaching to £500 (2400 dolls.) a year; and there is not the smallest doubt that those who want to make money and care nothing for the intellectual quality of their work should steadily follow this branch of "commercial journalism," which is more and more absorbing the journals devoted to women's interests and pleasures. Set against the dozen or so of women doing serious work of a literary character, such as essay writing, leaders, descriptive impersonal articles, and reviewing, there are hundreds who are writing up the shops, fashions in dress, the furnishing of houses, the toilette, and so forth, all of which specialities can be used for the advancement and profit of the advertisement department. It is, however, essential that the journalistic novice should embark upon her career clear-eyed, with a knowledge of the conditions prevailing in the market—upon which matters I claim the ability to be of some use in this little volume — and with definite aims and methods of workmanship. If you are a penniless bread-winner, it is not practical good sense, nor is it conducive to success, to limit yourself to reviewing and literary essays, until you find yourself middle-aged and in want, and follow this up by bitter laments that editors do not invite you to contribute to the lucrative chit-chat that fills their pages.

If, then, I were asked to sum up my advice to the beginner, it would be as follows: Take up one or more expert subjects. Dress, employments, complexion, what you will (so long as it is *in demand*), and make your name known as an authority thereon; but, at the same time, *refuse nothing* which you can do without dishonour. I do not pretend that this is consistent with elevated taste and culture; but I am here addressing the woman who must make a fair income if she is to live in any degree of comfort and refinement, and who sensibly acknowledges to herself, maybe not without a pang, that she cannot *afford* to reform the "journalistic stable." Let her make up her mind from the start that she must supply the commonplace needs of a commonplace reading public. I can assure her that, provided she have the usual education of the modern middle-class girl, the average share of quickness, swift, accurate observation, and the faculty for presenting her matter in readable form (which latter comes for the most part with practice), she will be able, with ordinary luck and within a couple of years, to make a fair income—as incomes of working-women go. Five years of diligent work ought to secure her some regular work which, with extra contributions, will bring her income up to about £120 (576 dolls.) a year, exceeding that of the average "high school" teacher, and supposed to be one on which a woman of refinement can live in decent comfort. The few technicalities of the craft, which mainly consist in a knowledge of the different journals with their special needs and characteristics, are of too elemental a character to present any difficulties to the most modestly endowed person; and the capacity for light chatter on shops, dress, society, &c., and the thousand and one trivialities which are the stock-in-trade of the woman journalist, grows and improves by practice.

It cannot be denied that the all-round journalist has a considerable degree of physical wear and tear. She must be up betimes, alert for several hours of the day, whilst she is chronicling private views, weddings, bazaars, and other functions, compelled to take her meals irregularly and to keep late hours; and until she has a berth with a modest salary, the strain on the nerves, the anxiety as to the future, with the dread of falling ill before any savings are accumulated, have a disastrous effect on the whole feminine

organisation.   In this respect she compares un-
favourably with the school teacher or the Civil
Service clerk. But she has one obvious advantage
over the former in that her work increases in
value as her name gets known, and she has not
necessarily to face the disqualification of being
"too old at thirty-five." In place of the deadly
monotony and mechanical drudgery of the
clerk, she has constant variety of work and scene,
contact with all sorts and conditions of men and
women, and opportunities through meetings, lectures, and visits to charitable institutions, of
getting to know something of the deeper side of
life; whilst for the frivolous there are, in the dis-
play of fine clothes, in the shoulder-rubbing with
fashionable people, in the glimpses of smart and
animated life, endless channels of interest and
pleasure.

❀ ❀ ❀

PART II.

EMBARKING ON JOURNALISM.

EVEN the seasoned and successful journalist would be perplexed as to the most useful counsel to be given on this head. Probably in the future the necessity for some kind of apprenticeship, which would have the effect of raising the journalistic standard, will be recognised; but as at the present time no training schools of any value exist, the best preparation for actual work is the ordinary all-round education which most girls nowadays get in the high schools.

Let us suppose that a girl of eighteen who has just left school, is compelled to become a bread-winner. She is facile with her pen, has gained perhaps literature prizes, and is generally attracted, so far as she knows anything of the employment, to the work of the journalist. Although it would be safe to say that any quick and fairly intelligent sixth form high school girl could transform herself into the average journalist by industry, practice, and the exercise of her intellect, yet it is necessary to say that there are certain qualities—to be found in a greater or lesser degree in everybody—which do materially contribute to the success of the journalist.

Quickness of Eye an Essential.

It is essential that the woman journalist—who will sooner or later have descriptive reporting to do—should have quickness of eye. Almost all women have an instinctive gift for taking in the details of dress at a swift glance, and this is a most useful, nay indispensable, part of the equipment of the average woman journalist. If the journalistic novice finds that she is almost entirely without this swift apprehension of trifles, and if a few months' practice does not give her a command of the faculty, she had better take up some branch of journalism which in no way depends upon quick observation and the capacity, so to speak, of mentally focusing things. In short, she must not hope to be a good descriptive reporter.

Another Important Qualification.

One may almost lay it down as an axiom that journalism should be avoided by those who think very slowly—find careful reflection absolutely necessary before writing half-a-dozen words —and are incapable of writing an article in the easy, light fashion that they would a letter. Of course, here again this faculty improves with practice, and becomes almost mechanical; but it is doubtful whether it ever goes with intellect of a really superior order; and one of the most intellectual women of my acquaintance — philosophical, highly cultured, and a clear-headed thinker—after a year's practice of light journalism, finds herself incapable of writing a trifling article without taking great pains.

But taking for granted the possession of quick, accurate observation, facility in arranging ideas, combined with the ordinary middle-class school education, a girl is sufficiently justified in believing that she has the preliminary equipment with which to start on her career of journalist.

Branches of Journalism.

The next important step is the choice of one or more special branches of journalism from the beginning. Many prominent journalists have drifted from reporting into reviewing, and from descriptive scraps about anything into one expert branch; but such would very likely admit that they would have done better to make their names steadily known from the beginning in the particular branches in which they later found success. There are many reasons for this. Take the chronicling of weddings, bazaars, and fashionable functions generally. The needy bread-winner, in the belief that this kind of journalism is easy and remunerative, sets herself to send in paragraphs relating to these topics to the society and

women's papers.   After a time she finds out what
her experienced sister could have told her, viz.,
that this social work is the most expensive and
least profitable for a poor novice journalist.
Why?   For two reasons.   Because nearly every
society and women's paper has a crowd of
regular and occasional contributors, the latter
often persons actually moving in good society, and
glad to advertise the social fêtes of their friends
for no payment at all; and because—a still more
important point, to which attention is never
called—unless she have a number of pretty and
fashionable dresses in which to appear at society
entertainments, or to extract information from
drapers, shopwalkers, and dressmakers, she will
find her position extremely unpleasant, and beset
with difficulties which may injuriously operate on
her work.   The novice who must begin earning
something at once, and cannot fall back upon her
father or husband for her dressmaker's bill, would
do well to avoid the rôle of society journalist at
the beginning of her career.

Reviewing.

The beginner will do equally well to abandon
all thought of reviewing, which is the prize of
the journalistic profession, and sought after by
University men of high distinction.   She may
get what goes by the name of "book notices";
but these are paid, in the inferior journals, at

" sweating prices," and as a stepping-stone to reviewing of a cultivated kind no more disastrous
method could be conceived. Reviewing can, as a
rule, only be secured through a literary reputa-
tion or by intimate acquaintance with an editor.
I shall have something more to say on this point
further on; but, so far as practical training is
concerned, the " noticing " of illiterate books in
cheap journals is wholly bad. What, then, are
the varieties of journalism which offer themselves?

Reporting.

This, although very hard work, entailing late
hours, irregular meals, and much travelling about
in trains, &c., seems to offer a good field for the
energies of active, capable women. Numbers of
charities and societies are concerned wholly
or mainly with the interests of women; and they
prefer to have a woman reporter at their meetings,
if she is able and sympathetic. Very few ladies
are attached to journals as regular reporters
in the same way that men are. I know of only
two attached to the staffs of important newspapers.
Neither of these ladies is a shorthand writer; and
as there is little likelihood—and many of us think
with good reason—of women being admitted as
Parliamentary reporters, there does not seem to
be any particularly good reason for devoting two
or three years to becoming expert at shorthand.

Unless meetings, &c., have to be reported verbatim, for which space can hardly ever be found,
a report giving faithfully the whole sense of a
meeting, however condensed, is infinitely more
useful and truthful than a verbatim report of one
or two speakers' speeches, with many important
points of other speakers left untouched for want
of space.

Reporting, therefore, seems to offer a good opportunity for careful, accurate journalists, capable
of giving a faithful impression of things. Practice will enormously increase the young journalist's capacity in this respect, and she should
take every opportunity of making herself
expert.

How to Practise Reporting.

The novice should go to meetings, come home
and make her report, and compare it next day
with the one in the *Times*, or some other good
daily paper. Sermons, lectures, and the like
can all be practised in this way; and it is quite
wonderful how quickly a little practice enables
one to present a lucid, coherent report. Once
one has become an adept in this kind of
journalism, it is no very difficult matter to get
stray reports accepted, but much more difficult
to get sufficient work taken during the first year
or two to make £50 (240 dolls.) a year or even
less.

The outsider's best chance of getting any notice taken of her reports, is to select events or things which are not sufficiently known or important enough to attract the staff reporter, and yet of interest. For instance, items of educational interest are frequently used by the *Manchester Guardian* in its London letter; and the *Echo* gives an unusual amount of space to philanthropic matter, and both depend largely on outside contributions. Many local meetings are of national interest, and there are a whole host of events relating to the welfare of women which might find space in the women's journals and columns overcrowded to-day with society gossip, if they were presented in an attractive manner by the woman reporter.

Let the young journalist keep her eyes open for any matter of this kind, weave it into a short report—from 300 to 500 words would be about the limit—and send a couple of slightly varied versions to two of the best women's journals. She might also send another report, slightly differing, to one or other of the big provincial papers; but she should avoid those (of which more detailed particulars will be found in another part of this book) which have a large number of regular London correspondents covering the entire ground. She had better, at this preliminary stage, invest in a Press guide, and expend five or six shillings in the purchase of provincial journals, with a view to finding out what fields still remain unworked. If she steadily furnishes good reports, some of which are sure to be accepted, getting her name known to editors as a reliable writer, she can await her opportunity for offering her services when some important affair occurs—a temperance or woman's congress, or an educational or Poor Law conference, of which the report is likely to be read largely by women—with a good chance of having her services accepted, and the way paved for more permanent work. But she should keep her eye so far as possible steadily fixed on the first-rate journals; and unless sheer necessity compel her, resist the temptation to send in paragraphs anywhere, no matter how vulgar the quality of the journal—an epithet which I think justly applies to many of the low-class "society" journals.

In pointing out this branch of journalism, it would not be fair to avoid reference to its disagreeable side, viz., the necessity it entails of going about late at night and into all sorts of places. Often, too, nearly always in evening meetings, the journalist has to take down her report to the office, so that her return home may be postponed till very late at night. It is extremely desirable for the reporter to live within walking distance of Fleet Street, and as this condition would cut off many girls from living with their families, and necessitate the barren, lonely, and terrible life of lodgings, reporting should only be taken up after careful consideration of these points.

How Copy should be Presented.

"Copy" is the name given to the journalist's MS., and the advice given here with regard to news applies pretty generally to all copy. This should be invariably written on one side of the paper only. It is not necessary to fasten leaves together, but they should be numbered in the right-hand corner; and the reporter who will not have the advantage of seeing her contribution *in proof*, should make a point of writing very legibly, otherwise endless time is lost—a very serious matter in newspaper offices. In almost all but daily journalism, the journalist is given a printed slip of his article, which he corrects prior to the corrected version appearing in the paper or magazine. Instructions on correcting proofs are given in Part IV.

A convenient size paper to use is the ordinary MS. sermon paper, and it is advisable to keep to the same size of sheet, as it saves the trouble of counting one's words.

Some papers prefer typewritten copy, and a few make this a *sine quâ non;* but provided the writing is readable at a glance, the novice need hardly ever go to the expense of having her work typed. Of course, if she possess a machine, she should

make use of it, and thereby probably ensure an
earlier reading of her MS. than would otherwise
be the case.

The average length of an article varies from 700
to 2000 words; but, roughly speaking, 700 words
for a daily paper article, and about 1500 for
articles in weekly and miscellaneous journals,
would be approximately correct.   The young
journalist should not exceed this number, at any
rate in the beginning, and much practice is required in order to concentrate one's ideas into this
limited space, which is, indeed, part of the art of
journalism.   Reports, descriptions, &c., are often
much shorter, and "About 500 words" is a very
frequent editorial injunction, whilst paragraphs
run from 100 to 300 words.

In sending an article for the first time the journalist should exercise care and discretion.   The
pages of the journal for which the paper is
intended should be carefully studied, the style
noted, whether popular, designed for semi-
educated persons, or for cultivated readers only,
the length of the articles observed, and, in short,
one's "literary coat cut accordingly." It is no
use sending articles which the writer knows
to be cultured in the hope that the editor
of a more or less illiterate popular journal
will gladly and gratefully accept them.   The
editor knows his public; he is paid by his
proprietor—sometimes a business man without

either the capacity to educate readers or the desire to do anything but make money—to supply this public; and he will only accept contributions that fall into line with the rest of the periodical. MSS. should be sent folded flat, not rolled. They should bear the name and address of the writer on an outside blank sheet; and also, as a protection against mischance, on the last page, and they should be accompanied by a very brief communication, conveyed after this fashion :—

To the Editor of the *English Journal.*

SIR,

    I am forwarding herewith an original article of mine called "Kites." May I beg you to give your careful consideration to the same with a view of its being published in your journal, and in the case of non-acceptance to return it to me with as little delay as possible.

I am, Sir,

Yours faithfully,

——— ———

It is advisable to enclose a stamped, addressed envelope to ensure the return of the article in case of non-acceptance. But my own experience on this point is, that however unsatisfactory editors may be with regard to delay in replying and in inserting articles, they almost invariably return MSS., whether stamps are enclosed or not. The most harassing part of the unattached journalist's life is experienced in the uncertainty which is inseparable from this period; and that is why I earnestly counsel the bread-winner to

endeavour as strenuously as possible to get some
work, a column, or even half a column, that is
regular. And for this reason—notwithstanding
one gentleman who insists that £600 (2880 dolls.)
a year is easily earned by writing for the magazines—I strongly advise those who are solely de-
pendent upon their earnings to leave magazine
work alone, until they have advanced a little way
upon their career and have some income, however
small, upon which they can count.

Articles which are of no current interest are
often held over for months, and even for years,
by magazine editors, and payment upon publication only is almost invariably the rule. In
many cases, however, no objection is raised to
payment on acceptance, and one of the best
paying of the magazines, and that generously
opens its pages to the new-comer (the *Strand*)
has never, so far as my knowledge goes, refused
to pay upon acceptance, if this condition is re-
quested by the contributor. This, I think, is all
that need be said here about the details of
" copy."

Specifically Feminine Subjects.

Even more suitable for women than reporting
is the field offered by feminine subjects, such as
household economy, practical dressmaking, advice
on dress, cookery, house furnishing, and women's
employments, in all of which the woman journalist

has an immense advantage over her male rival.
However much one may deplore the preponder-
ance of these matters in the Press, it cannot be
denied that they are capable of being treated in
a most useful manner, and of furnishing inexperienced but busy women readers with most valuable information. Unfortunately many of these
columns are in the hands of amateurs, who do
much harm by their extravagant advice upon
dress, and by their ignorant and absurd counsel
on cookery and household management; and
unless a girl be willing to study any of these
special subjects she cannot possibly carry out her
work carefully and conscientiously.

Numbers of young women, however, know how
to make neat, well-fitting clothes, and with this
fundamental capability, the theory of dressmaking can be acquired with sufficient accuracy to
enable them to play the rôle of dressmaker
journalist with success. There is an immense
field for this function in the cheap papers read
by tradesmen's wives, milliners and middle-class
women generally; and I confidently expect that
before long, instead of elaborate descriptions of
costly trousseaux and shooting and ball dresses,
which are quite beyond the purses of such readers,
we shall have simple lessons with diagrams in
dressmaking, such as have already made their appearance in one or two quarters. Especially is
this needed for working women, who are worse off

than any other class as regards instruction of this
kind. Of course, the theory of dressmaking for
the purpose of journalism must be studied just as
carefully as it would be for County Council
lectures. But, as at present there are probably
not more than a dozen journalists who can give
this excellent simple instruction, the opening is
better than that for the teacher, and the writer's
income would probably be doubled, even trebled,
as the value of her services got known.

In connection with dress, there is also the more
overcrowded field of purely æsthetic treatment as
distinguished from the practical point of view.
The journalist fulfilling this function is supposed
to have good taste—a qualification which is frequently lacking, if we may judge from the illustrations given—and a knowledge of what things
are being worn and at which shops they are to be
purchased. I think the young journalist would
find more difficulty in getting this kind of dress
journalism. It largely consists of answers and
advice, necessitating some kind of connection with
the drapers advertising in the journals wherein
the contributions appear. It is desirable for the
"dress adviser" to have some elementary knowledge of dressmaking; she must also know how
to describe the contents of the shop windows at-
tractively, so as to excite the interest and envy
of her readers, and she must have some idea of
the specific points concerning fashionable dress,

and the manner in which these points are described.

Much the same training as that already spoken of for dressmaking is involved in writing upon cookery and household management and needlework; and if in the case of the last-named the journalist can furnish simple sketches in illustration of her ideas, she is pretty sure not to lack work. How useful this kind of journalism can be, may be seen by a study of the excellent practical articles and advice published in *The Bazaar*.

Women's employments about which a terrible flood of imperfect and sometimes erroneous information is poured forth, is also a most suitable subject for feminine treatment, and if handled by a woman who is honest, impartial, and expert, can be of the utmost value to inexperienced women needing work.

Musical and Art Criticism.

This branch of journalism is, for the most part, even in the sixpenny women's papers, for some extraordinary reason, almost wholly in the hands of men, and offers an interesting though limited field for a cultivated writer's taste, imagination, and knowledge. Dramatic criticism involves attendance at first nights, and also some of the disagreeable features inseparable, apparently, from the stage. But as an enormous number of concerts take place in the afternoon, and as nearly all art shows can be visited in the daytime, it seems strange that so small a number of women are employed as art and musical critics. A large number of lady journalists attend private views and concerts, and describe the people and frocks, and everything but the artistic productions; but their functions are not those of the trained critic. Seeing what a number of cultivated women musicians there are, this want of enterprise is striking; and I cannot help thinking that students who have a thorough knowledge of the theory of music, might do worse than qualify themselves as critics. The best way to bring herself under the notice of editors would be for the young critic to write a short magazine article dealing with some aspect of the musical art in an original and individual way; and with this object, it would be best to get her views printed in a journal that is not an exclusively musical organ.

Miscellaneous Contributions.

In addition to the branches of journalism that I have named, with a few others, such as sport and athletics, church matters, &c., about which it is not necessary to go into detail, and all of which ought to involve a fair degree of skilled knowledge, there are a whole host of miscellaneous articles which almost anyone with sense, industry,

and intelligence can write, and that are more
particularly required by the all-round weekly
periodicals. One can hardly say that any kind
of training comes in for work of this sort, beyond
dexterity in arranging matter in a light, attractive fashion. A whole host of papers, of which
Tit-Bits may be taken as representative of the
very best standard, buy miscellaneous articles
from outsiders, that are made up for the most
part of facts strung together with light, easy
narration. Details of royal people, royal resi-
dences, descriptions of any places that are of
interest for the moment, or of industries or armies
or ships, or public performers, or of a thousand
every-day and out-of-the-way subjects, are acceptable if they form light reading, and are compiled
in a popular form. Many persons, however sedu-
lously they practise this kind of journalism, fail
to become expert and to bring themselves in re-
quest amongst editors for supplying the com-
modity, whilst others find the task easy, and are
able thereby to secure a comfortable income, and
almost by instinct they come to utilise almost
everything that crosses their path.

Short Stories.

There is another branch of journalism, hardly
to be dignified by the name of authorship, yet not
journalism in its strict technical sense, that almost
more than any other offers an excellent means of

livelihood to those who have the inventive faculty required for story telling.

The demand for short stories and serial stories suitable for newspapers, novelettes, &c., is enormous, and likely to increase rather than diminish. I know a woman not yet thirty, of mediocre talents, whose name is quite unknown to the literary critics, yet who makes a regular income of £300 to £400 (1440 to 1920 dolls.) a year by supplying novelette fiction. She insists that the work is regular, plentiful, and well paid, and that once one's name gets known to half-a-dozen editors, there is hardly any difficulty in getting sufficient orders to ensure a good income. Although hard and exhausting, especially when the writer is engaged upon long novelettes, the work has the advantage of being carried on at home, enabling a woman bread-winner to give some attention to her domestic affairs during the day.

The lady I have mentioned advises those anxious to sell their stories, to take half-a-dozen different kinds of journals and to study the length of tales appearing in them and the particular class of readers to which they appeal; although she thinks there is no great difference in the essential qualities and conditions characterising all these productions. She started with a short story in the *Family Herald*, and almost immediately afterwards wrote a novelette on similar lines, which was accepted by another well-known penny journal. Domestic stories with a good deal of short dialogue and melodramatic incidents, about which the love story of the hero and heroine is interwoven, usually find a ready sale. Just at present, the pseudo-historical romance being in favour, she is busy concocting tales to meet the prevailing fashion, which, however, she predicts will not last long; whilst the domestic tale with love incidents and mild melodrama is perennially in fashion.

Unfortunately, the authority we have cited does not feel able to give any precise hints as to how a woman could train herself to produce these stories; but she asserts that a study of the conventional tales to be found in dozens of provincial journals, coupled with a certain amount of flexibility and faculty for grouping stories round well-worn situations, is pretty nearly all the equivalent needed. Here also is some additional advice furnished by this story writer:—

"The length of the short stories should be about 3,500 words. The serials are generally from 20,000 to 60,000. Each chapter in the serial story should be a distinct advance in plot, and should leave off at a point sustaining interest and curiosity. All 'problems' should be scrupulously avoided, and the purveyor of this kind of fiction should not attempt any kind of character drawing. The villains should be villains, and 'act

accordingly,' and complexities of motive, character, and feelings, such as are essential to better
art, must be severely left alone.   The writer
should bear in mind that so far as any art is concerned, the reading public for these stories is in
the most elementary stage of development, and
she should always ask herself, Would this story
interest the average fairly intelligent shop girl?
For, though the literary wares we produce are by
no means limited to the shop girl purchaser—
many of the novelettes and papers in which they
appear being regularly read and bought by wives
of professional men, actresses, society women, and
the rest—still, this is a tolerably correct intellectual calibre by which to judge.

"The stories should be laid preferably in high-
class life, though there is no objection to making
the heroine of the humbler class, companion or
governess, or the hero of the professional class,
barrister or doctor.   But tales dealing with the
lives of the working class or tradespeople are not
popular, and are more difficult to dispose of.   Of
course, I do not pretend that this kind of writing
has any connection with literature.   It is simply
a means of earning a livelihood, and if pure and
innocent in intention and achievement, is, I think,
a quite harmless one.   It enables me to keep
a comfortable home for myself and an invalid
sister, whereas had I continued writing magazine
stories and novels, of which I am the author

of five, I should be still wretchedly poor, and my sister would be in a charitable institution.

"One last hint. The young authoress should enclose with her MS. serial a short summary of the plot. If an editor or syndicate manager likes this summarised plot, half the battle is won. The National Press Agency, Tillotson's, of Bolton, and one or two other similar agencies give good prices for stories, and so far as my experience goes are entirely honest and reliable."

Novel-writing and Authorship Generally.

I do not propose to go into the different modes of publishing novels here, as any useful examination would need more space than is possible in a small manual; and there is the less necessity for data of this kind, as they can be obtained in the most trustworthy fashion by anyone choosing to pay a guinea and belong to the Incorporated Society of Authors, 39, Old Queen Street, Westminster, S.W.

It seems to be a pretty unanimous opinion that novel-writing is a very precarious mode of obtaining a living, and that for the first five or six years after the publication of an even moderately successful novel, the author had better have some other means of living. A successful writer of girls' stories tells me she is convinced that there is a good opening for short stories suitable for young people, such as are printed in the *Strand Magazine*, the *Royal*, *Cassell's Saturday Journal*, &c., and that deal with adventures and school life. Healthy, bright stories for young women are badly needed, the cheap periodical fiction being for the most part insipid love tales, badly conceived and badly written.

Stories translated from the French and German and Italian do not sell readily unless they are sensational, or have a special interest, and, moreover, payment for them is very inadequate.

Educational Literature.

There are, however, better prospects for well-educated women, especially those who have had a classical education, in the shape of editing and compiling school books. Several publishers, notably Messrs. Blackie, Simpkin, Marshall and Co., Macmillan, and Constable, make a speciality of educational literature, and women who have any definite ideas to offer should apply to one or other of them. It is a waste of time, irritating to both parties, to write vaguely expressing a desire to do work on the chance of a publisher needing the services of the writer, seeing that this important personage is pretty sure to have a staff of employees upon whom he can rely, and whom he is likely to prefer to a stranger. But the case is different when the stranger has a scheme of her

own to put forward, which if good is certain to
receive consideration.

Technical Articles for Trade Journals.

With the exception of the journals devoted to
dressmaking, the trade publications are not
largely contributed to by women journalists, no
doubt because they involve a technical knowledge that few women are likely to possess.
Yet there are a considerable number of trades
and occupations—laundry work, farming, gardening, and so forth—which have aspects of special
interest to women : and I feel convinced that there
is an opening in these departments for women
writers who have had expert training, and who
would perhaps find writing about these occupations more profitable than following them! Nor
need these articles be exclusively confined to
purely trade journals. There are a whole host
of publications taken by farmers and artisans,
whose wives would most thankfully read expert
articles written with especial reference to the
capabilities of women, on the laundry, dairy
work, poultry-keeping, flower gardening, and the
like. Yet how rarely does one come across any
such series of articles written simply, lucidly, and
with practical knowledge. For these trade
articles the pay is good, and at any rate at
present, as far as women are concerned, the field
is less crowded than most other branches of

journalism. Great attention to detail would be needed, as women's operations for the most part are on a small scale, involving a small outlay of money and small profits; and the instructions must be of an uncomplicated nature, owing to the few opportunities that women have of learning the technicalities of machinery, apparatus, and trade processes in general.

Where the Outsider has her Chance.

The advantage of successful journalism of the miscellaneous kind is that it can be carried on whilst a woman is living at home in the country, though there is no doubt that accessibility to the British Museum is helpful. Moreover, the "outsider" has every bit as good a chance as the member of the staff, and having, as a rule, more time, and being to a certain extent fresher, she can often get her work into papers when her more experienced, but at the same time more hackneyed, rival fails.

It is not possible here to particularise all the journals that are open to "outsiders." Moreover, an exhaustive list with details of remuneration is given in Part V. of this handbook, and further particulars are given in the "Writer's Year Book" (published at 1s. 6d.). A few hints as to the kind of wares that should be offered will probably be found useful by those who prefer laying themselves out to provide

three or four miscellaneous articles a week, even
though this kind of work is attended with uncertainty, both as to being accepted at all, and,
when accepted, as to date of publication and payment. Still, there will be a large number of
women anxious to remain at home who will find in
the supplying of miscellaneous articles a pleasant
and fairly profitable mode of earning a livelihood.

The *Evening Standard* prints a miscellaneous
article every evening which exactly fills a column.
The precise length is of great importance, and you
must be careful to count the exact number of
words, which I do not specify here, as the size of
the type and spacing may be at any time altered,
but which a careful examination of a recent issue
will easily yield.

Now, as regards subjects. Interesting customs
worked up into a readable narrative, indeed any
subject lending itself to a new point of view containing not *views*, however, but facts, will have
a good chance of acceptance. An early
article of my own was on Old School Books, and
I well remember the pleasure I felt on the night
it appeared, on hearing a well-known Professor
say (it was, of course, unsigned, and he had not
the remotest idea that he was speaking to the
author), " What an amount of information, and
how well arranged! " Of course, I had " got
up " a good deal of the information, but I had

also handled some of the old books, and I suppose
my knowledge and my interest in the subject combined to make it a good article.
Another of my articles was on the Portraits in
the Portrait Gallery, and here my facts were at
my fingers' ends, for a weekly visit to this interesting place has been my practice all the time
I have resided in London.

Do not suppose that London offers any advantages so far as saleable facts are concerned: on
the contrary, you who live in the country are
surrounded by all sorts of things considered
"interesting" by the modern editor.   Villages
with very old inhabitants, villages with curious,
interesting industries, the ways of gipsies and
hoppers, that you can yourself observe, interesting gardens, and so forth, are all raw material.
For the *Evening Standard*, I should say, get a
fresh first-hand subject of present-day interest,
and weave round it, judiciously interspersed with
narrative, all sorts of facts and statistics that
bear on it.

The *Globe* "Turnover," so called because it
runs on to the second page, is quite a journalistic
institution. Almost anything that is capable of
being treated with the peculiar kind of *badinage*
that *Globe* readers favour, will serve as a subject.
Statistics are not required, but rather a whimsical
way of dealing with an everyday idea.

As, however, the *Globe* "Turnover" is the subject

of much attention, I advise you to turn yours, at any rate at first, to such journals as *Great Thoughts*, which accepts short half-column literary and general papers—for instance, any interesting facts about the birth-places or burial-places of great writers or artists, details about interesting philanthropic institutions, and so forth. Statistics are not needed. A pleasant, descriptive article of about 700 words with an occasional illustration can often find acceptance there, and if the journalist will be satisfied with a wide circulation for her article in place of generous payment she gets it.

Cassell's Saturday Journal, Pearson's Weekly, and similar popular weeklies, require more lively, or what the Americans call "live," matter than *Great Thoughts*. Articles for these journals must contain anecdotes, facts, information, all strung lightly together, and calculated to make no demand on the intellect. Curious sign-boards of inns, old shops, odd names, the thousand-and-one things that the average mind is interested in, well-got-up information about the ways of detectives, and any other "sensational subject" will all work into the kind of article that is wanted. Nearly all these papers pay £1 1s. to £2 2s. (5 to 10 dolls.) for an article, and if you lay yourself out to purvey this class of goods you will soon get an instinctive knowledge of the articles that are saleable.

Do not waste time and exertion on the *Speaker,
Spectator, Athenæum,* or *Saturday Review.*
Speaking generally, they do not accept articles
from outsiders, though a specially clever or
original article on a literary or social theme, has,
I have found, a good chance of acceptance.

If your genius lies in the "snippet" article,
a thing that is hardly more than a note, and you
are able to hit upon the tastes of the average
commonplace person, there are a whole host of
papers such as *Home Notes, Woman's Life,* &c.,
which will readily purchase from the outsider.
Seasonable topics usually find treatment in this
type of weekly.   By this I mean New Year's
Customs, Leap Year Proposals, Valentines, and so
forth.   The pay is about the ordinary rate, £1 1s.
(5 dolls.) a thousand words, and in the beginning,
whilst one is trying to make a name, 10s. 6d.
(2½ dolls.) here and 15s. (3½ dolls.) there, come in
very opportunely.

Short domestic stories, either melodramatic or
turning on some phase of simple love, are required
by all the women's cheap penny papers; and if
you have any turn for this sort of thing, which
requires a real instinct for what this type of reader
likes, be sure and cultivate it, as no vein is more
profitable.

News of the moment, without photographs, is
bought by the *Daily Mail,* which is very partial to
"outsiders," and with sketches or photographs

by the *Daily Graphic.* Nearly all the dailies have what they call a "magazine page," and for this they want all sorts of light stuff similar to that found in the women's papers. Scraps of personal gossip, popular fads and fancies, the prevailing modes in note-paper, pet dogs, dancing, and the like, form the theme of nine-tenths of the little articles or paragraphs of which these pages consist.

PART III.

THE JOURNALISTIC MARKET.

ALTHOUGH in journalism, as in all other occupations, the laws of supply and demand must be learned by experience, still, a few useful hints may be given to the novice as to the nature and requirements of the different journals, which may save her much time, money, heartbreak, and expenditure of energy. I will assume that the young journalist has had some little training and practice in the particular line of writing which she intends to pursue.

The next question is how to get her goods placed on the journalistic market. This, one may take occasion to remark, is a slightly more difficult matter than writing the article. A year or two ago, someone made the simple calculation that as it was quite easy to write 3000 words a week, and as the lowest rate of pay was £1 1s. (5 dolls.) per thousand words, therefore even the inexperienced journalist could easily make £3 3s. (15 dolls.) a week! She could easily make four times £3 3s. a week upon these premises, which are wholly misleading and absurd. The number of articles one can dispose of does not happen to be identical with the number of articles one can write; and this reasoning, applicable to any industry, is peculiarly so to journalism, for almost all editors have an immense accumulated stock, upon which they can draw when they do not wish to expend money in purchasing new articles.

It is specious arguments of this kind that have made women rush into journalism, regardless of the injury they do to the genuine bread-winner, who lives by her earnings, and cannot afford to work for 5s. (1¼ doll.) a column. This small remuneration is, however, ample for a woman whose presence in the journalistic market is due, not to necessity, but to vanity—to the desire to have it known that she "writes for the papers," or to a wish to get free entrance to entertainments, and lastly to the need of another £15 or £20 (72 to 96 dolls.) a year for her millinery bill. It is to be hoped that with the purer, newer journalism of the future, some sort of trades unionism will come into force, if only for the benefit of the legitimate woman journalist, who finds herself cruelly handicapped to-day by the selfishness of her well-to-do sisters.

Meanwhile, the market being as it is, the novice must take such prices as she can get, and try as speedily as possible to make known the value of her work, so that she can command better

terms. With one or two exceptions, the women's
papers pay wretched prices for casual contributions, and as little as 7s. 6d. (1 doll. 80c.) for 1000
words is given by two or three publications.
In the beginning of her career, this is no more
than the inexperienced journalist can expect, and
there is just this to be said: in no other trade
or profession in the world would a comparatively
unskilled person be able to earn anything at all
until she had gone through two or three years'
apprenticeship. Of course, part of the apprenticeship of the journalist is learning how to dispose of her wares to advantage; and as the pain-
fulness of this period may be lessened by advice
from the seasoned, experienced hand, I shall now
indicate in which quarters the different varieties
of productions may be sent, giving such additional details as seem to me likely to be
profitable.

News and News Agencies.

Suppose, then, that the young journalist lays
herself out to provide news in the shape of paragraphs, short descriptive accounts, and reports.
Now, there are certain items of news that are of
almost universal interest, and certain to find
acceptance in the daily and weekly newspapers.
Any little bit of intelligence connected with the
Queen, for instance, is " good copy." Let us suppose our journalist is staying near Sandringham,

and learns that the Queen has paid a visit
to an old servant. If she can elicit from the
favoured individual what the Queen said and any
other similar details, she can make up a quarter-
column account—which would be in most newspapers about 400 to 500 words or more — and
send it off instantly to one or more of the daily
or evening newspapers, or—still better, because
more advantageously paid—to one or other
of the news agencies. These news agencies
act as distributors, and the interesting contribution would be sent out simultaneously to scores
of London and provincial journals. The National
Press Agency, Whitefriars House, Carmelite
Street, Fleet Street, London, E.C., deals honour-
ably and fairly liberally with all its contributors;
and a really good paragraph will bring in from
7s. to 15s. (1½ to 3½ dolls.).

There are hundreds of everyday affairs which
can be utilised in this way by a clever, alert
journalist, who must, however, always ask herself: Is this event likely to attract the presence
of the professional reporters attached to newspapers and agencies, or is it likely to go un-
noticed, and afford a suitable opportunity for my
efforts? This discrimination must be exercised
personally by each journalist who is unattached,
and it becomes more exact with experience
and general knowledge of the newspaper
world.

News, to be of value, must be fresh and accurate, and though during the last four years we have seen for the first time in this country a chain of systematic lies accepted by some of the lower-class papers, there is a growing feeling against this practice on the part of the more intelligent of the public, and the conscientious journalist should do all in her power to ensure her intelligence being trustworthy.

Light news relating to country weddings of well-known personages, social festivities, and the doings of prominent women, will find ready admission into the ladies' journals, and both the *Ladies' Field* and the *Lady's Pictorial* pay fairly well, and — what is equally important — very punctually. These women's journals, as well as one or two others, will also accept matter that is not simply chatter and gossip about high-class people. They are glad of items about the doings of interesting women, and in some papers, the *Lady* for instance, special columns are reserved for the doings of women in all classes of activity.

It must be remembered that none of the women's journals pay so highly for news as the news agencies, but they will frequently take paragraphs which the agencies could not utilise; and when crowns or dollars are of vital importance, it is useful to know that the light society journals, which largely depend upon outside contributions, and also many of the other women's journals which I have not named, but which any journalist can easily find out for herself, offer a likely market.

Miscellaneous Contributions.

Now as regards the articles to which I have already referred as "miscellaneous." These need not be topical, as news must be, and they are not of necessity useless if rejected by one journal, as a whole class of journals make use of much the same material, and only differ in name, outward appearance, and the place of publication. If the articles are connected with some topic of interest at the moment, they have a better chance of being used quickly, and as delay is always a drawback to a young writer, she should make her contributions as far as possible of current interest. For instance, of late an enormous amount of attention and interest has been directed to the Japanese, and anyone who could produce fresh, bright, light articles on the manners of those interesting people—"How the Japs Woo and Wed," "How the Jap Child Plays," and so forth—could have found a ready sale for them in such papers as *Tit-Bits*, and the host of other publications that are akin to *Tit-Bits*, such as *Answers, Pearson's Weekly, Cassell's Saturday Journal*, &c. An article of this kind should not be more than 1500 words in length, and if the journalist can produce a photograph or two she might send her copy to an illustrated paper, the *Daily Graphic, Sketch, Black and White,* or the *Penny Illustrated,* and get as much as £3 3s. (15 dolls.) for the seasonable contribution.

The journalist who intends to purvey these miscellaneous articles, either written at first hand, or compiled from other magazines or books, will find that a very moderate capacity for taking a rough photograph will help enormously. A number of editors are largely influenced in their acceptance of articles by capability for illustration, and a decision on this point is greatly helped by a couple of rough sketches, or simple photographs. Hosts of travel articles that sound hackneyed and stale can be invested with a new interest, in editorial eyes, by the sight of an attractive photograph, however amateurish this may be; and as the number of daily, weekly, and monthly illustrated journals is rapidly growing, I cannot help thinking that she who has some little dexterity with the camera with which to show off her literary wares to the greatest advantage, will have a decidedly better chance than those who ignore its value.

Miscellaneous articles, which serve for such a weekly as *Tit-Bits* or *Great Thoughts* (the remuneration offered by the latter journal is scarcely one-half that of the former, which pays from £1 1s. (5 dolls.) per column, and often, if not invariably, allows 2000 words for a readable article), can often be legitimately expanded into a good magazine article with the addition of illustrations. I will give an instance from my own experience. A few years ago the editor of a trade journal commissioned me to collect some statistics about the doll industry in this country and abroad. In the course of my investigations I came across a large amount of information of no use to a trade journal, but of distinctly popular interest. These interesting data I arranged in a readable form, and got the article accepted by an evening journal, which has every evening an instructive miscellaneous article (for this it pays £2 2s.—about 10 dolls.); and finally, seeing the additional light and attraction that pictures would give the subject of "Dolls and Doll-making," I procured more details of various kinds and published a long article in the *Strand Magazine*, for which I received £10 10s. (50 dolls. 40c.).

The *Strand, Pearson's Magazine*, and the *Pall Mall Magazine*, which pay from £8 to £15 15s. (38 to 75 dolls.) for an article of 4000 words, should be aimed at in preference to the smaller magazines, which pay very poorly. The *Windsor* pays less highly than the *Strand*, but, like this magazine, it will pay generously for any article specially *apropos*. It is no more trouble to write an article for the *Strand Magazine* than for the *Leisure Hour*, and the pay of the former is double, often treble, that of the latter, which, in common with all the religious magazines, pays rather inadequately.

In addition to miscellaneous articles, all these miscellaneous journals like articles dealing with distinguished persons of popular interest, great painters, actresses, and so forth; and though these have been somewhat overdone of late years, any prominent man or woman who possesses anything unique in the way of talent, or wealth, or beautiful pictures, or horses, or houses, can be woven into an article that with illustrations need not long go begging.

Short Stories for Cultivated Readers.

Stories which can be included under this head are not quite so easy to dispose of as the illiterate, popular kind. Many of the more high-class magazines have a little circle of contributors upon whom they draw month after month, to the detriment of the journal and to the great weariness of its readers, who would gladly see fresh names and fresh ideas in its pages. *Longman's Magazine* is almost entirely supported by regular contributors, and the unknown writer, however clever her work, would, I think, have little chance of acceptance there. *Macmillan's Magazine*, with a far higher literary standard, has a wider literary outlook, and the obscurity of the author is no bar to the acceptance of her work if it be good enough. The very best stories that ever appear in this country are to be found in the pages of *Macmillan* (the beginner should study such exquisite little gems as "A Page of Philosophy," and a perfect little masterpiece called "The Little Marquis," by the late Hannah Lynch, which is only equalled by Stevenson's short stories), and any woman whose style is delicate and polished, and whose stories satisfy the conceptions of an artistic mind, could not do better than submit her stories to the editor of this magazine. From 3000 to 4000 words would be long enough, and payment varies from £10 to £16 (48 to 76 dolls.). Less exalted, although far higher than many other high-class magazines, is the standard of *Temple Bar*, and many of its stories are contributed by unknown writers, prices varying from £5 to £10 (24 to 48 dolls.).

Good stories from the French or German, turning on military episodes of a highly dramatic kind, will often find acceptance in the *Windsor* or *Strand*, or *Pearson's;* but they must be very dramatic and stirring, and are not easy to produce of a suitable length.

Women's Columns.

The contributions known as women's columns, made up of scraps of social gossip, dress, and the like, are features of many of the London daily and weekly and the provincial papers, and are

but slowly giving way to matters of a more intelligent nature. The article of this order which
appears every week in *Truth* is generally considered to be a model of its kind, and those who
wish to excel in this department of journalism
could not do better than bestow upon it their
earnest attention.

Generally speaking, these columns are remu-
nerated at "sweating" rates, the average being
about 15s. to £1 1s. (3½ to 5 dolls.) for a letter
amounting to one and a half, two, or even three
columns, whilst a large number fetch 7s. 6d. or
10s. 6d. (1¾ or 2½ dolls.) for the same amount
of work. A few women who introduced the idea,
or who have made their names known in connection with this speciality, receive better payment; but even they find it necessary to do half-
a-dozen columns, in as many different journals,
in order to make an income that is regular and
adequate. The single word to be said in favour
of this journalism is its regularity, and even 7s.
(1 doll. 68c.) a week regularly will be a substantial
help towards the rent of the struggling wage-
earner.

The new writer will find herself bewildered
when she comes to consider the best opening
for her services. Almost every journal seems
provided with something in the way of light
feminine gossip, and the one that is not, it may be
safely assumed, will have many a time been

bombarded by anxious contributors. Nevertheless, there are new journals constantly appearing, which are generally announced beforehand, giving the newcomer a chance to proffer her services, and this she must take care to do in *definite shape.* Further, there are many important provincial journals—the *Manchester Guardian,* to name only one—which have no regular women's column, and may some day give more space to matters of interest to intelligent women.

How successful a page of this sort can be was shown a few years ago, when the *Daily Chronicle,* under the editorship of Mr. Massingham, devoted a page once a week to every kind of matter of value and interest to women of intellect and culture; and its discontinuance has been a real loss not only to daily journalism, but to scores of women who do not ordinarily buy a daily paper.

The *modus operandi,* then, would be to watch for new journals, and to endeavour to persuade any editor who has not yet provided himself with such matter, that he would find it interesting and attractive, more especially if not entirely composed of gossip about society and the fashions. By way of making the proposal less alarming, it is well to suggest that the column might appear monthly at first, and oftener if successful. As I have said, these contributions are not paid for at particularly profitable rates, and there is little

E

likelihood of the prices rising, as many of the syndicates and agencies supply letters on women's topics at 5s. (1 doll. 20c.) and 10s. (2 dolls. 40c.) apiece, adequately satisfying papers which do not require individual or characteristic contributions. But it is an immense gain for the struggling journalist to get any kind of regular work.

If the journalist endeavours to compete with the agencies I have just named, she must first be able to show original matter, and, secondly, so to negotiate affairs that she is able, with but slight variation, to insert her letter in two or three distinct places—say a provincial journal and a London evening paper or a Scotch newspaper. If she takes care that the papers are not read by the same set of people, she will rarely find her editors raising any objection to this method. It is well to fix a modest price at the start, as few editors of journals which are at all flourishing will refuse to give more generous terms if the contribution prove to be a popular feature with readers. For a letter of this kind contributed by a newcomer 15s. (3½ dolls.) for 1000 words would be fair pay, and if the writer intends to make her living by this sort of work, she should sign her name or take a distinctive, telling pseudonym —in contradistinction to the Daisys, Lady Marys, and so forth, which are so plentiful nowadays— and keep to it. If, however, she means to do *better* work, the striking pseudonym or real name is undesirable, and would do harm rather than good.

Disposing of Essays.

Where to send essays—that is, articles of a literary or social nature, written in a polished and finished form—is the anxious question of many young *littérateurs* seeking to do work of a more literary kind; and very difficult it is to give any exact counsel on this point. Nearly all the really high-class reviews have an adequate staff, and imply that they do not want MSS. from outsiders; yet it is absolutely certain that well-written articles which are at all striking and brilliant have a good chance of acceptance. The writer of these words had some articles relating to the "Care and Education of Feeble-Minded Children" accepted by the *Times* when her name was wholly unknown. The articles were accurate, based on statistics, and broke fresh ground, and they were paid for at the rate of £3 3s. (15 dolls.) a column! The *Saturday Review* occasionally takes essays, mostly of a serious nature dealing with some educational or philanthropic or literary matter, from casual contributors. New weeklies, too, are sometimes started which give outsiders a chance, the short-lived but wonderfully brilliant *Review of the Week* having mainly depended upon unknown writers. Most editors, it may be safely stated, are on the lookout for original well-written essays.

The rate of pay in these instances is often not high—an article of 1000 words would probably not fetch more than £1 1s. (5 dolls.)—but it gives the new writer a capital chance of showing her talents, and if she is really clever she may be sure that her essays will attract the notice of editors and lead to further work. Such articles must be sparkling and elegant; and as there is some strain in turning out little essays of this kind, it is probable that two, or at most three, a month will involve more effort and brain fag than the young writer can afford to expend.

Literary essays of a much inferior kind, and generally didactic in their nature, are accepted by the *Sunday at Home, Good Words,* the *Sunday Magazine,* and *Great Thoughts.* The last-named, as I have before hinted, does not pay well, about £1 or £1 10s. (4½ to 7½ dolls.) being the average for a page article; but it has a big circulation and this recommendation—that it allows contributors to sign their names, thereby giving unknown ones an opportunity of gaining publicity.

Long, purely literary articles are becoming more and more difficult to get published, and, with the exception of the *Contemporary* and *Fortnightly,* scarcely any of the high-class reviews publish more than an occasional article, written by a distinguished *littérateur,* every few months. If the unknown journalist wants to get into the best of the reviews, such as the *Nineteenth Century* or the *National*, she must choose some subject of striking popular interest, not too serious and heavy, yet not purely frivolous—one in which the subject and its treatment will compensate in the eyes of the editor for the obscurity of the writer. This has been my own experience in the two or three articles I have had published in the *Nineteenth Century*, and the payment is so liberal— as much as £25 (120 dolls.) being given for an article of 4000 words—that the subject is worth expending a good deal of thought, time, and trouble over.

One thing has always to be remembered in connection with magazines, and this is that they go to press, that is, are printed, weeks before their appearance. The consequence is that many events of real interest are useless for magazine purposes, partly because descriptions will long before have appeared in the illustrated weekly journals, and partly because after three or four months have elapsed the interest in any event will probably have vanished.

All these points, and how many more! must be individually learned by each journalist, and even the fullest and wisest advice is only supplementary to, not a substitute for, personal experience. In these pages I think the novice will have learned what can be indicated about the training for journalism, the preparing of various MSS. and their placing on the journalistic market. Pages might be added on the proper manner of interviewing, on style, on the opinions of persons making £800 (3840 dolls.) a year by magazine work, and on kindred matters. But as each person with any individuality will have her own style of writing, and her own method of interviewing; and as, in my judgment, the only dicta one can give as regards the former are simplicity and clearness, and with regard to the latter accuracy and good taste, I should waste space here by entering into the discussion of methods which each journalist must work out for herself. The best advice that the seasoned journalist can give is in the form of a few general principles, coupled with some practical knowledge of the journalistic market, and this, I hope, I have succeeded in doing.

❀ ❀ ❀

PART IV.

CORRECTING PROOFS.

In correcting a proof the novice should keep in view one great rule that applies to all classes of journalism: make only such alterations as are absolutely necessary. The article, paragraphs, notes, or what not, should receive all the trimming-up they may require (the sub-editor will see to the *trimming-down*) while they are in manuscript. This will entail no expense, and very little trouble. It is only natural that to the young journalist contributions assume in print a somewhat different appearance from that they had when they left the pen; but every correction made in the type means expense, and there is no surer way of exasperating the members of the editorial staff or of incurring the wrath of the proprietor than by making a host of frivolous corrections.

In these days of Linotype machine-composition, every correction means resetting a whole line at least, as the machine does not set separate types, but casts each line in a solid piece of metal, technically called a "slug," and this obviously

cannot be corrected in the manner that obtained
with hand-composition. The insertion of a couple
of words will often cause the resetting of a whole
paragraph, and, in addition to the cost of this,
there is the question of loss of time to be taken
into account—always a serious matter on a
journal. The practised writer avoids "tinkering"
a proof, not only because she has acquired the art
of expressing exactly in writing the ideas that she
wishes to convey, but also because she knows
that mere synonymic alterations do not make
matters any clearer to the reader, nor the
journalist's contributions more welcome to the
editor.

In articles of any length some amount of
alteration is often not only desirable but necessary.
It may be that since the manuscript left the writer
some time has elapsed before she receives her
proof, and if it be a topical article something may
have happened in the meantime that will render
corrections essential. On provincial journals, too,
some printers' errors may have escaped the proof-
reader's eye, and these, if noticed by the writer,
should, of course, be marked.

No matter how ignorant the young journalist
may be of printers and their methods, it is desirable that she do not exhibit this when it can be
avoided. She should familiarise herself with the
proper method of marking any corrections that
may be essential. To assist her in this matter I

TEXT MARKS.	EXPLANATIONS.	MARGINAL MARKS.
[	Next line.	*N.P. or Par.*
(triple underline)	Capitals.	*Caps.*
(double underline)	Small capitals.	*S. C.*
(single underline)	Italics.	*Ital.*
~~even~~ or	Delete (omit).	(delete mark)
~~course~~	Leave as printed (a word accidentally scratched out).	*Stet.*
"	Put in inverted commas.	(mark)
funny ⌐ it is ⌐	Transpose.	*trs.*
ꞑ or ꞑ	Replace n by u; w by W.	u / — W /
⋏	Leave space between words.	#
———	Insert a lead.	*lead*
⋏	Insert rule.	/ —— /
greatest blessings. ⌐ ⌐ During wet days	Run on; the same paragraph.	*run on*
ꞇꞇꞃ	Reverse position.	9
fun	Broken letters.	X or *br. lr.*
king	Wrong fount of type.	*w. f.*
⋏	Put full stop.	⊙
⋏	Insert letter h.	h /
in ⌣ deed	Bring together.	⌒
B⌒ooks	Place in straight line.	(double line)

Marks used by Proof-readers and Journalists.

tabulate on page 57 the text and marginal marks used by proof-readers and editors. No correction should be marked in the text without the corresponding mark being plainly made in the margin. Tiny marks in the text alone would stand a chance of being missed by the printer: he follows the marginal corrections, the text marks simply showing him to what parts they apply. A reference to the accompanying Plate will show the novice exactly how a proof should be corrected; but, of course, she must never expect to receive from any journal a proof bristling with errors like that which has been "prepared" for the illustration. The same piece of matter, corrected by the printer, is reproduced on page 59.

Some of the marks on the Plate are self-explanatory, but a few words may perhaps elucidate others. The matter being a quotation, it is put in inverted commas (known to printers as "quotes"). "France" is the first word of the article, so it is printed in small capitals ("s.c."), that being the style of the journal for which the matter is intended. In the second line "l.c." means that the D should be a small d, that is the letter in the compositor's "lower case." (Two cases are used by the hand-compositor—the lower contains the small letters, punctuation marks, and spaces; and the upper accommodates the capitals, small capitals, figures, accented letters, &c.) The black mark in the third line is a space sticking up. The word "of" is doubled in the fifth line; the "delete" (omit) mark is made in varying

"FRANCE—where so much has been done in recent times to advance a knowledge of the merits of the old Cremonese makers, and especially as she has produced (partly as a result of her researches) the greatest violin-maker that has lived since Joseph del Jesu died—might well have claimed the place of honour after Italy. Early references to the violin seem to be as meagre in the literature of France as they are in that of any other country, and it is chiefly from paintings and accounts of *fêtes* that any knowledge concerning its history there can be derived.

"There is a picture, painted about 1485, called the 'Psaultier du Roi René,' containing a figure playing upon a viol which approaches the violin in shape, having a circular sound-hole in the centre. This René fought in Italy in 1482 in conjunction with the Venetians, against the Duke of Ferrara, and, as he was a great patron of the fine arts, it is supposed that he brought this instrument or its design from the latter country."

The matter on the accompanying Plate corrected.

ways, but all traceable to their source—*d/*. A "lead" (space between the lines) has been omitted after the fifth line; while after the last line but

five there is a lead too much. "Stet" (eighth
line) is the Latin for "let it stand"; the word
"the" has been erased in error. Dots are placed
under the wrongly-deleted word. Words or letters
that are out of their proper order have a line drawn
round them, as in the seventh and twelfth lines,
and "trs." is marked in the margin. The words
"There is a picture" should commence a new
paragraph. Titles of pictures are generally placed
in inverted commas, but as the example shown is
already a quotation, only single inverted commas
are used. In some journals it is customary to
place quotations or extracts within single inverted
commas; had that style been adopted in the present instance, then "Psaultier du Roi René"
would have been correctly placed within double
quotes, thus: 'There is a picture, painted about
1485, called the "Psaultier du Roi René," containing a figure,' etc. A line or two lower the
hyphen has been omitted from "sound-hole."
The abbreviation "w.f." means wrong fount: the
V in "Venetians" (last line but four) is of a
different "fount" or pattern of type. In the same
line a space is required between "Duke" and
"of." In the last line but one, a roman ("rom.")
m is required in place of the italic letter. The
meaning of the remaining corrections is fully set
forth on page 57.

One more item of advice before closing this
chapter. If the young journalist find a number

of words, a whole sentence, or even several paragraphs missing from her proof let her not grumble
at the printers for making mistakes, and
laboriously re-insert the missing matter. There is
no mistake except on the part of the writer, and
the result is that the editor's blue pencil has been
at work.

PART V.

LITERARY REMUNERATION.

In the preceding pages I have given some information as to the amounts paid for various kinds of contributions, from which the young journalist will have gained some general idea as to what may be expected for acceptable work. In the case of specially-commissioned articles, or of contributions by experts in particular subjects, there is, of course, practically no limit as to the amount paid; indeed, many journals have no fixed rates, the remuneration being purely a matter of arrangement between writer and editor, and it is, therefore, impossible to give details. I am, however, enabled to give below a fairly representative list of British and American journals and magazines, with the rates paid to "outside contributors," and other useful information as to length of articles and stories.

A correspondent in New York sends me the following very interesting and informative letter on the subject of journalism in the States:—

"A New York magazine publisher who has had considerable experience in publishing in

London, tells me that as a general rule the American magazine publishers pay just about twice the rates paid by English publishers for contributions.

"American magazines pay a minimum rate of 5 dolls. to 10 dolls. (£1 0s. 10d. to £2 1s. 8d.) a page for acceptable articles, and from that as high up as they have to go. The rates paid to star writers are often very high. Mr. Grover Cleveland, formerly President of the United States, and who is not at all a literary man, is said to have been paid 1000 dolls. for a short article which recently appeared in the *Saturday Evening Post.* Miss Hegan, a new literary light who recently made a hit with 'Mrs. Wiggs of the Cabbage Patch' and 'Lovey Mary,' could no doubt get 10,000 dolls. (£2083 6s. 8d.) for a serial story from any of the leading magazines. The minimum rate on the *Century Magazine* is 10 dolls. (£2 1s. 8d.) a page. The same company also publishes *St. Nicholas Magazine,* in which the minimum rate is 8 dolls. (£1 13s. 4d.) a page. Some magazines pay by the word, and the price ranges on the good publications from 1c. (½d.) a word up. The lowest rate on *Collier's Magazine* is 2c. (1d.) a word. *Collier's* has been running a series of Sherlock Holmes stories, for which they paid Sir A. C. Doyle 60c. (2s. 6d.) a word: this is said to be the top-notch figure. Rudyard Kipling can get about 25c. (1s.) a word here. Richard Harding Davis, a well-known American writer,

can get 15c. (7½d.) a word. When it comes to the
stars it is simply a matter of bargain and sale,
and this applies to newspaper as well as to magazine articles. Of course, there have been cases,
and perhaps many of them, where writers have
been glad to get into print without receiving any
pay. I am also told that writers, or their friends,
have actually paid certain publications for
accepting an article.

"In the newspaper field in New York payment
for space is about as follows per column:

The *New York Herald*...........$7.00 (£1   9s.   2d.)
The *New York World*...........$7.00 (£1   9s.   2d.)
The *Evening Telegram*...........$5.00 (£1   0s. 10d.)
The *Evening Mail* $4.80 (£1.)
The *Sun* $8.00 (£1 13s.   4d.)
The *New York Journal* $7.00 (£1   9s.   2d.)
The *New York Times* $6.00 (£1   5s.   0d.)
The *Evening Post* $5.50 (£1   2s. 11d.)

" These are the minimum rates, and, as a rule,
the maximum rates also. The *Sun*, which is said
to be the leader in this country from a literary
standpoint, pays the largest minimum, as you will
observe, but it rarely pays anything higher than
the minimum; while other dailies, the *Journal*
more particularly, sometimes pay very large sums
to special correspondents, such as war correspondents.

"As a rule the best paying positions on the
New York dailies are those connected with the

business department. Journalism is rapidly becoming more commercial all the time. The selling prices of publications of all kinds have come down and down. This, of course, makes it necessary to get the revenue from advertising. The advertising manager, it follows, then, is an important man. The circulation manager is also an important person, and both of these have grown in usefulness somewhat at the expense of the editorial and news man.

"New York rates, of course, set the pace for the rest of this country, and the publishing business is rapidly centring here. Boston probably comes next, Philadelphia third, and Chicago fourth. Some Chicago men have recently been making strong efforts to establish some high-class periodicals in that city, with not much success as yet."

British and American Newspapers and Magazines, and their Rates of Remuneration.

Amateur Gardening.
7s. ($1.68) per col.—Office, 148-149, Aldersgate Street London, E.C.

Answers.
From £1 1s. ($5.4) per col.; £3 3s. ($15.12) per short story.—Office, Carmelite House, London, E.C.

Army and Navy Gazette,
From 10s. ($2.40) per col.—Office, 3, York Street, Covent Garden, London, W.C.

Athenæum.
15s. ($3.60) per col. (about 770 words).—Office, 11, Bream's Buildings, Chancery Lane, London, E.C.

F

Bazaar.

Long articles, 11s. 6d. ($2.76) per 1,000 words; short articles (up to 500 words), notes (100 to 300 words), and paragraphs (30 to 100 words), 15s. ($3.60) per 1,000 words.—Office, Bazaar Buildings, Drury Lane, London, W.C.

Bicycling News.

25s. ($6) to £2 2s. ($10.8) per page (1,600 words).—Office, Lucifer House, Lionel Street, Birmingham.

Black and White.

£1 11s. 6d. ($7.56) per 1,000 words.—Office, 63, Fleet Street, London, E.C.

Blackwood's Magazine.

From £1 ($4.80) per page.—Office, 45, George Street, Edinburgh.

Boudoir.

From £1 1s. ($5.4) per 1,000 words; special rates for commissioned articles.—Office, 54A, Fleet Street, London, E.C.

Boy's Own Paper.

From £1 1s. ($5.4) per page.—Office, 65, St. Paul's Churchyard, London, E.C.

Bystander.

£1 10s. ($7.20) per 1,000 words; photographs 10s. 6d. ($2.52) and £1 1s. ($5.4) each; drawings also used.—Office, Tallis Street, London, E.C.

Cassell's Saturday Journal.

£1 1s. ($5.4) per col.; special page at £5 ($24) per page.—Office, La Belle Sauvage, Ludgate Hill, London, E.C.

C. B. Fry's Magazine.

From £1 11s. 6d. ($7.56) per 1,000 words; articles dealing with every phase of outdoor life required.—Office, 12, Burleigh Street, Strand, London, W.C

Century Magazine.

Usually about £2 2s. ($10) per 1,000 words.—Office, Union Square, New York.

Chambers's Journal.

£1 11s. 6d. ($7.56) per 1,000 words.—Office, 47, Paternoster Row, London, E.C.

Chic.

From £1 1s. ($5.4) per col.—Office, 3, Arundel Street, Strand, London, W.C.

Church Family Newspaper.

From £1 1s. ($5.4) per article.—Office, 111, Fleet Street, London, E.C.

Citizen.

£2 2s. ($10.8) per col.—Office, Throgmorton House, 15 Copthall Avenue, London, E.C.

City Press.

£1 1s. ($5.4) to £1 11s. 6d. ($7.56) per article.—Office, 148, Aldersgate Street, London, E.C.

Collier's Weekly.

Usually about £2 2s. ($10) per 1,000 words.—Office, 416-24, West Thirteenth Street, New York.

Connoisseur.

Usually 15s. ($3.60) per col. (of about 500 words).—Office, 95, Temple Chambers, Temple Avenue, London, E.C.

Cornhill Magazine.

£1 ($4.80) per page (about 420 words).—Office, 15, Waterloo Place, London, S.W.

Cosmopolitan.

Usually about £2 2s. ($10) per 1,000 words.—Office, Irvington-on-Hudson, New York.

Daily Chronicle.

From £1 1s. ($5.4) per 1,000 words; short paragraphs (200 to 250 words), 1½d. per line.—Office, Fleet Street, London, E.C.

Daily Express.

From £1 1s. ($5.4) per 1,000 words.—Office, 15, 17, Tudor Street, London, E.C.

Daily Mail.

From £1 1s. ($5.4) per 1,000 words.—Office, Carmelite House, London, E.C.

Daily News,

From £1 1s. ($5.4) per 1,000 words.—Office, 19-22, Bouverie Street, London, E.C.

Daily Telegraph.

From £1 1s. ($5.4) per 1,000 words.—Office, 135 and 141, Fleet Street, London, E.C.

Dental Review.

From £1 5s. ($6) per 1,000 words.—Office, 413, Marshal Field Building, Chicago, U.S.A.

Dublin Review.

6s. 3d. ($1.50) per page.—Office, 28, Orchard Street, London, W.

Echo.

Short articles and sketches, £1 1s. ($5.4) per 1,000 words.— Office, 19, St. Bride Street, London, E.C.

English Illustrated Magazine.

£1 1s. ($5.4) per 1,000 words ; £1 1s. ($5.4) per drawing ; 5s. ($1.20) per photo.—Office, 25, Hart Street, London, W.C.

Evening Mail.

About £1 ($4.80) per col.—Office, 203, Broadway, New York.

Evening News.

From £1 1s. ($5.4) per 1,000 words.—Office, Carmelite House, London, E.C.

Evening Post.

About £1 3s. ($5.50) per col.—Office, Broadway, New York.

Evening Standard.

£2 2s. ($10.8) per article.—Office, 103-105, Shoe Lane, London, E.C.

Evening Telegram.

About £1 0s. 10d. ($5) per col.—Office, Herald Square, New York.

Farm and Home.

From 12s. ($2.88) per col.—Office, 17, Furnival Street, London, E.C.

Field.

From £1 1s. ($5.4) per 1,000 words.—Office, Bream's Buildings, Chancery Lane, London, E.C.

Fortnightly Review.

£1 ($4.80) per page (articles of 4,000 to 5,000 words preferred).—Office, 11, Henrietta Street, Covent Garden, London, W.C.

Frank Leslie's Monthly.

Usually about £2 2s. ($10) per 1,000 words.—Office, 141, Fifth Avenue, New York.

Free Lance.

From 10s. ($2.40) per col.; much more for commissioned work.—Office, 15, Essex Street, Strand, London, W.C.

Gentlewoman.

From £1 1s. ($5.4) per col. (about 1,000 words preferred).—Office, 70 to 76, Long Acre, London, W.C.

Girl's Own Paper.

From £1 1s. ($5.4) per 1,000 words.—Office, 65, St. Paul's Churchyard, London, E.C.

Globe.

£1 1s. ($5.4) to £2 2s. ($10.8) per article of about 1,200 words.—Office, 367, Strand, London, W.C.

Golden Stories.

£10 ($48) to £20 ($96) per story (about 20,000 words).—Office, Carmelite House, London, E.C.

Graphic.

£1 10s. ($7.20) per 1,000 words.—Office, Tallis Street, London, E.C.

Great Thoughts.

About £1 (4.80) to £1 10s. ($7.20) per page.—Office, 4, St. Bride Street, London, E.C.

Harper's Magazine.

Usually about £2 2s. ($10) per 1,000 words.—Office, Franklin Square, New York.

Hearth and Home.

7s. ($1.68) to 10s. ($2.40) and upwards per col.—Office, 10, 11, Fetter Lane, London, E.C.

Home Circle.

£1 1s. ($5.4) per page.—Office, Carmelite House, London, E.C.

Home Companion.

£10 ($48) to £20 ($96) per story (about 18,000 words).— Office, Carmelite House, London, E.C.

Home Notes.

From £1 1s. ($5.4) per 1,000 words.—Office, 17, Henrietta Street, Covent Garden, London, W.C.

Horner's Penny Stories.

£20 ($96) to £25 ($120) per story (about 18,000 words).— Office, Carmelite House, London, E.C.

Hour Glass (formerly the *Golden Penny*).

From £1 5s. ($6) per 1,000 words; photographs 7s. 6d. ($1.80) and 10s. 6d. ($2.52) each.—Office, Tallis Street, London, E.C.

Household Words.

From £1 1s. ($5.4) per 1,000 words.—Office, 8, Whitefriars Street, London, E.C.

Illustrated London News.

£2 2s. ($10.8) per 1,000 words.—Office, 198, Strand, London, W.C.

Lady's Realm.

> From £1 5s. ($6) per 1,000 words.—Office, 34, 36, Paternoster Row, London, E.C.

Land and Water.

> From £1 5s. ($6) per 1,000 words.—Office, 12, 13, Henrietta Street, Covent Garden, London, W.C.

Leisure Hour.

> From £1 5s. ($6) per 1,000 words.—Office, 4, Bouverie Street, London, E.C.

Lloyd's Weekly Newspaper.

> £1 11s. 6d. ($7.56) per col. (articles or short stories).—Office, 12, Salisbury Square, London, E.C.

London Magazine (Harmsworth's).

> From £2 ($9.60) per 1,000 words.—Office, Carmelite House, London, E.C.

M.A.P.

> £1 ($4.80) per 1,000 words ; commissioned work, from £2 ($9.60) to £4 ($19.20) per 1,000 words.—Office, 17, 18, Henrietta Street, Covent Garden, London, W.C.

McClure's Magazine.

> Usually about £2 2s. ($10) per 1,000 words.—Office, 141, East Twenty-fifth Street, New York.

Macmillan's Magazine.

> From £10 ($48) to £16 ($76.8) per story of 3,000 to 4,000 words.—Office, Macmillan and Co., Ltd., St. Martin's Street, London, W.C.

Madame.

> From £1 1s. ($5.4) per 1,000 words.—Office, 8, Essex Street, Strand, London, W.C.

Mail and Express.

> Usually about £2 2s. ($10) per 1,000 words.—Office, 203, Broadway, New York.

Manchester Despatch.

From £1 10s. ($7.20) per column.—Offices, Withy Grove, Manchester (head), and 92, Fleet Street, London, E.C.

Methodist Recorder.

From 10s. 6d. ($2.52) per col. (2,000 to 4,000 words, with illustrations preferred).— Office, 161, Fleet Street, London, E.C.

Morning Advertiser.

From £1 1s. ($5.4) per 1,000 words.—Office, 127, Fleet Street London, E.C.

Morning Leader.

From £1 1s. ($5.4) per 1,000 words.—Office, Stonecutter Street, London, E.C.

Morning Post.

From £1 1s. ($5.4) per 1,000 words.—Office, 346, Strand, London, W.C.

Munsey's Magazine.

Usually about £2 2s. ($10) per 1,000 words.—Office, 111, Fifth Avenue, New York.

National Review.

From £1 ($4.80) to £5 ($24) per page.—Office, 37, Bedford Street, Strand, London, W.C.

New Liberal Review.

From £1 1s. ($5.4) per 1,000 words.—Office, 82, 83, Temple Chambers, London, E.C.

New York Herald.

About £1 9s. 2d. ($7) per col.—Office, Herald Square, New York.

New York Journal.

Usually about £2 2s. ($10) per 1,000 words.—Office, 162, Nassau Street, New York.

New York Sun.

About £1 13s. 4d. ($8) per col.—Office, Park Row, New York.

New York Times.

About £1 5s. ($6) per col.—Office, Park Row, New York.

New York World.

Usually about £2 2s. ($10) per 1,000 words.—Office, Pulitzer Building, Park Row, New York.

Onlooker.

From £1 1s. ($5.4) per 1,000 words.—Office, 16, Bedford Street, Strand, London, W.C.

Outlook.

£1 5s. ($6) per 1,000 words.—Office, 109, Fleet Street, London, E.C.

Pall Mall Gazette.

From £1 1s. ($5.4) per 1,000 words.—Office, Newton Street, High Holborn, London, W.C.

Pall Mall Magazine.

From £2 ($9.60) per 1,000 words.—Office, Newton Street, High Holborn, London, W.C.

Pearson's Weekly.

From £1 1s. ($5.4) to £3 3s. ($15.12) per col.—Office, 17, 18, Henrietta Street, Covent Garden, London, W.C.

Photogram.

From £1 ($4.80) per 1,000 words.—Office, 6, Farringdon Avenue, London, E.C.

Pictorial Magazine.

From £1 1s. ($5.4) to £2 2s. ($10.8) per 1,000 words.—Office, Carmelite House, London, E.C.

Political Science.

8s. ($1.92) per page (4,000 to 7,000 words preferred).—Office, 9, St. Martin's Lane, London, W.C.

Punch.

From £2 ($9.60) per 1,000 words.—Office, 10, Bouverie Street, London, E.C.

Queen.

From £1 5s. ($6) per col.—Office, Bream's Buildings, London, E.C.

Realm.

From £1 1s. ($5.4) per 1,000 words.—Office, 6, Essex Street, Strand, London, W.C.

Regiment.

7s. ($1.68) to 10s. ($2.40) per col. of 600 words.—Office, 7-15, Rosebery Avenue, London, E.C.

Reynolds's Weekly Newspaper.

From £1 1s. ($5.4) per col.—Office, 1, Arundel Street, Strand, London, E.C.

Royal Magazine.

From £1 11s. 6d. ($7.56) per 1,000 words.—Office, 17, Henrietta Street, Covent Garden, London, W.C.

St. James's Gazette.

£1 5s. ($6) per 1,000 words.—Office, 15, Dorset Street, White-friars, London, E.C.

St. Nicholas Magazine.

From £1 13s. 4d. ($8) per page.—Office, Macmillan and Co., New York.

Saturday Review.

£3 3s. ($15.12) to £4 4s. ($20.16) per article.—Office, 33, Southampton Street, London, W.C.

Scribner's Magazine.

Usually about £2 2s. ($10) per 1,000 words.—Office, 153-157, Fifth Avenue, New York.

Sketch.

£1 10s. ($7.20) per col.—Office, 198, Strand, London, W.C.

Smart Set.

From £2 2s. ($10.8) per 1,000 words.—Office, 92, Fleet Street, London, E.C.

Spectator.

£5 5s. ($25.20) for a good article.—Office, 1, Wellington Street, Strand, London, W.C.

Sphere.

From £2 2s. ($10.8) per 1,000 words; topical photographs and drawings liberally paid for; articles only to be submitted at editorial request.—Office, 6, Great New Street, E.C.

Standard.

From £1 1s. ($5.4) per 1,000 words.—Office, 103-105, Shoe Lane, London, E.C.

Star.

£1 1s. ($5.4) per short story (about 1,500 words).—Office, Stonecutter Street, London, E.C.

Strand Magazine.

£3 3s. ($15.12) per 1,000 words; very liberal terms for specially suitable matter.—Office, Southampton Street, Strand, London, W.C.

Studio.

From £1 1s. ($5.4) per page (2,000 to 4,000 words preferred).—Office, 44, Leicester Square, London, W.C.

Sun.

From £1 1s. ($5.4) per 1,000 words.—Office, Temple Avenue, London, E.C.

Sunday Chronicle.

From £1 5s. ($6) per 1,000 words.—Offices, Withy Grove, Manchester (head), and 92, Fleet Street, London, E.C.

Sunday Stories.

£10 ($48) to £15 ($72) per story (about 18,000 words).—Office, Carmelite House, London, E.C.

Tatler.

£1 1s. ($5.4) per 1,000 words; photographs 10s. 6d. ($2.52) and £1 1s. ($5.4); drawings also used.—Office, 6, Great New Street, Fleet Street, London, E.C.

Temple Bar.

From £5 ($24) to £10 ($48) per story.—Office, Macmillan and Co., Ltd., St. Martin's Street, London, W.C.

Tit-Bits.

£1 1s. ($5.4) per col. ; £2 2s. ($10.8) per col. on special page.—Office, Southampton Street, London, W.C.

To-day.

£1 1s. ($5.4) per 1,000 words.—Office, 8, 9, Essex Street, Strand, London, W.C.

Tribune.

Usually about £2 2s. ($10) per 1,000 words.—Office, 154 Nassau Street, New York.

Truth.

£5 5s. ($25.20) per short story ; 3d. per line in some cases.—Office, 10, Bolt Court, Fleet Street, London, E.C.

United Service Magazine.

From 5s. ($1.20) per page of about 400 words.—Office, Messrs. Clowes, Cockspur Street, London, S.W.

Vanity Fair.

From £1 1s. ($5.4) per 1,000 words (paragraph matter and short stories).—Office, Essex Street, Strand, London, W.C.

Weekly Budget.

About £1 ($4.80) per col. for articles ; stories by arrangement.—Office, Red Lion Court, London, E.C.

Weekly Dispatch.

From £1 1s. ($5.4) per col.—Office, 3, Tallis Street, London, E.C.

Western Druggist.

From £1 5s. ($6) per 1,000 words.—Office, 358, Dearborn Street, Chicago, U.S.A.

Westminster Gazette.

£2 2s. ($10.8) per 1,000 words.—Office, Tudor Street, London, E.C.

Windsor Magazine.

From £1 10s. ($7.20) per 1,000 words.—Office, Windsor House, Salisbury Square, London, E.C.

Woman's Life.

From £1 1s. ($5.4) per 1,000 words (stories of 2,000 words preferred).—Office, 3-12, Southampton Street, Strand, London, W.C.

World.

£2 2s. ($10.8) per 1,000 words.—Office, 1, York Street, Covent Garden, London, W.C.

World's Work.

From £1 11s. 6d. ($7.56) per 1,000 words.—Office, 20, Bedford Street, Strand, London, W.C.

Zoophilist.

From £1 1s. ($5.4) per col.—Office, 6, White Hart Street, Paternoster Square, London, E.C.

When photographs or drawings supplied by the journalist are used, they are in nearly all cases paid for.

A well-known journalist sends the following information :—" In addition to those enumerated in the foregoing list, there are many periodicals in British Dependencies and Colonies, and also in the United States, which offer a ready market for English contributors. Although most of them have London offices, the best plan is to submit work to head-quarters direct, as this saves considerable delay.

The following are among the most open of such journals in India and the Colonies :—

Pioneer (Allahabad).
Times of India (Bombay).
Indian Daily News (Calcutta).
Madras Mail (Madras).
Sydney Bulletin (Sydney, N.S.W.).
Melbourne Age (Melbourne Victoria).
Cape Times (Cape Town).
Cape Argus (Cape Town).

"The rates of payment vary in each case, and are, on the whole, somewhat below those obtaining in this country. Indian papers always settle their accounts in rupees, and as the loss entailed by converting them into sterling is not allowed for, the English contributor comes off rather badly when cashing her cheque. The usual scale of remuneration is from fifteen to twenty-five rupees (a rupee represents 1s. 4d., or 32c.) per column, and accounts as a rule are settled quarterly.

"In America the journalistic field is a wide one. It is also well worth cultivating, for the rates of payment are, generally speaking, considerably higher than those prevailing in England. American editors, too, have many other pleasing traits (from the point of view of the ' Free Lance ') not always shared by their British *confrères*. For one thing, they decide promptly whether they will use a contribution or not ; for another, payment is made at once in th event of acceptance. For ordinary matter the usual scale rate is from $10 (about £2 2s.) per 1,000 words, but very much higher terms are freely offered for anything of special interest. Among

the different periodicals best worth writing for in
the United States may be mentioned :

Scribner's Magazine.	*Collier's Weekly.*
Century Magazine.	*Cosmopolitan.*
Harper's Magazine.	*Mail and Express.*
Munsey's Magazine.	*Tribune.*
McClure's Magazine.	*New York Journal.*
Frank Leslie's Monthly.	*New York World.*

" Full addresses of the above will be found in
the list on pp. 65 to 77.

" The Free Lance who keeps her eyes and ears
open, and has what in journalistic circles is termed
a ' nose' for news, can earn a fair sum by con-
tributing topical paragraphs to the daily press.
Nearly every paper is open to outside contributors
for this class of work, and many of them set apart
considerable space every day for the publication of
such items. Prominent among these may be mentioned the *Daily Telegraph* (' London Day by Day'
columns), the *Westminster Gazette* (' Here, There,
and Everywhere' columns on the back page), and
the *Daily Chronicle* (' The Office Window' column).

" What is wanted most for these particular
features are short, bright notes, dealing with
persons and places occupying public attention at
the moment. There is also a good market for
informative paragraphs contributed to the ' London
letters' of the big provincial journals. Payment
ranges from 2s. 6d. (60 cents.) in the case of a few

lines, to 10s. 6d. ($2.52) for a more lengthy or
specially interesting note. The *Westminster
Gazette*, it may be mentioned, has a fixed scale of
3d. (6c.) per line.

"The many trade journals, both in this country
and America, that represent various industries, are
also quite worth the attention of the Free-Lance
journalist. Some technical knowledge of the subjects written upon, and the requirements of the
periodical they are submitted to, are, of course,
necessary. If these qualifications are lacking, the
contributor is almost certain to make serious mistakes. It is also not always safe to estimate the
nature of a paper by its title.

"The number of trade papers is very large, for
practically every imaginable industry has its own
organ. Some of these are extremely influential, and
can boast of enormous circulations. Their rates of
payment, however, are not lavish. A guinea ($5.4)
per 1000 words indeed, is the exception rather than
the rule. Fortunately, no very high standard of
literary excellence is insisted upon before admission
can be gained to their columns.

"Of the trade journals most open to chance contributors, the following are the principal :—

DRAPERS' RECORD.—Office, 155, Cheapside, London, E.C.
JEWELLER AND METAL WORKER.—Office, 24, Clerkenwell
    Road, London, E.C.
HARDWARE TRADE JOURNAL.—Office, 8, Finsbury Square,
    London, E.C.

LEATHER TRADES REVIEW.—Office, 24, Mark Lane, London, E.C.

GROCERS' MONTHLY.—Offices, 37, Shoe Lane, London, E.C.

WESTERN DRUGGIST.—Office, 358, Dearborn Street, Chicago, U.S.A.

DENTAL REVIEW.—Office, 413, Marshal Field Building, Chicago, U.S.A.

GROCERY WORLD.—Office, Philadelphia, U.S.A.

"Of the above, the *Western Druggist* and the *Dental Review* pay from £1 5s. (6 dolls.) per 1000 words.

"Of course, it is impossible—considering the number in existence—to give anything like a complete list of all the periodicals to which the outside contributor may send articles with a fair prospect of success. For all practical purposes, however, it may be boldly stated that every paper is open to everybody."

PART VI.

SOME PERSONAL EXPERIENCES.

An all-round journalist has furnished me with the following valuable expression of her own opinions and experiences:—

" I have read the foregoing pages [in MS.], and I do not take so pessimistic a view of journalism as an occupation for women as the writer. I think it offers work which for payment, pleasant variety, and easy conditions, compares very favourably with that in which other women are engaged. It is uphill work at the start, but a quick, well-educated woman can soon earn, without much training and experience, sufficient to keep her in bare board and lodging (that is, £1—4 dolls. 80c.—a week), and seeing the amount of learning and scholarship that barristers and doctors go through before they can make this amount, I don't think we can grumble. Then consider the fearful overwork of the high school teacher or nurse for ten or eleven months in the year, whose earnings are rarely more than £100 (480 dolls.) a year, whilst many journalists, with plenty of leisure, make £3 to £4 (14 to 19 dolls.) a week. I myself am an all-round journalist, able to report meetings, describe dresses and functions, put together descriptive articles for magazines; in short, I am useful, quick, and dependable, but neither brilliant nor literary.

"For some years, being neither wealthy nor influential, I had difficulty in making more than £1 10s. (7¼ dolls.) a week, but lately I was made one of the staff of a weekly journal, and my salary is £2 10s. (12 dolls.) a week, with plenty of time to make another pound or more. I do my work when and how I like, the sole condition being that my copy shall be good, and punctually delivered.

"When I see the tyranny to which governesses and nurses are obliged to submit, I count it a great gain that in journalism the woman is entirely her own mistress as regards the ordering of her life. She works, as a rule, for a male employer, who does not worry her or interfere with her, and she generally has time to be something more than the 'hack journalist'—time, that is, to perform some of the domestic duties which are the function and privilege of a woman.

"If I were asked to give one piece of pregnant wisdom to a young journalist, I would say to her,

G 2

'Dress well, and always look nice.' This may
sound very disagreeable in some ears, and may
seem to imply that one's success is due to ille-
gitimate methods, but that idea I do not mean
to convey at all. The work of the all-round
journalist, which is what nine out of ten women
must start with, involves coming into contact with
persons to be favourably impressed, and also with
male editors and male proprietors, who naturally
like their representatives to do them credit at
social functions. Then, again, editors—it is only
natural—dislike employing women who *look* very
poverty-stricken; therefore, worldly and wicked
as this advice may seem, I advise no journalist
to let it be known, except in very exceptional
circumstances, that she is a struggling bread-
winner. Advantage will instantly be taken of
her, and her confession will evoke not compassion,
but contempt. All chivalrous men with any right
feeling hate the idea of women taking part in
the fight and scramble for bread; and, strange
as it may seem, and mischievous as are the
results of this policy, they prefer to employ a
woman who is scribbling from any other reason
but dire necessity.

"I do not think myself that anything would be
gained by a sort of 'trade union,' perhaps because
I am enough of an individualist to hate the
pressure of numbers in any way. But much may
be done by tact and quiet explanation. For this

very post I have just received, I had a rival in the shape of a well-to-do woman who lives with her husband, a prosperous business man, in a West-End residence. I put these facts quietly before my editor, who seemed to see things in a new light, and he gave me the appointment, though the rich competitor has a far more widely-known name than mine.

"Another consideration that I would most strenuously urge upon the young journalist is to have some regard for her health, and, if possible, to get a mid-day meal. I know how difficult it is to manage this on £1 (4 dolls. 80c.) a week, especially if one must dress well; but I found it possible to avoid the terrible breakdown of nerves and health generally which makes the life of the mature journalist a misery, by pocketing my pride, and getting a wholesome meal—I will not say a *dainty* one—for 6d. or 7d. (12c. or 14c.) a day at one of the work-people's restaurants. It isn't pleasant to eat one's chop and potatoes, or steak, or mutton and barley, amidst unfastidious diners, in surroundings that offend one's delicacy and taste; but far better suffer this drawback and get a nourishing meal, than wreck one's physique on tea and buns or tea and buttered scones.

"As regards the actual work itself, though I agree that a woman would do best to specialise in one or two departments and get her name

known in them as an expert, still in the beginning, unless one has an income sufficient for
rent, this is sometimes impossible, and I advise
a young journalist to set herself to anything and
everything that comes in her way—sport, needlework, cookery, and what not. A good plan of in-
sinuating one's services is to ply some provincial
or local journal steadily with one's wares in the
shape of interesting detached paragraphs. One
can constantly hear of provincial journals suitable
for one's articles through friends resident in the
locality; and though the income gained will only
be a tiny one, still the beginning of profes-
sionalism is made, and that is much.

"I have tried my hand at *miscellaneous*
articles, but I do not find them encouraging or
profitable, unless, as you say, they are topical;
for they are often kept many months. The
Evening Standard is one of the few papers for
such articles; one is printed every evening, and
they are wonderfully entertaining and instructive.
It is not very difficult to get a couple in each
month after a little practice, with the aid of old
magazines and books at the British Museum; and
this means an income of £4 4s. (20 dolls. 16c.) a
month, though, of course, it is irregular, articles
being sometimes kept for a month or two (not
more, in my own experience). The length should
be about 1500 words, and the article should be
divided into three paragraphs.

"The question has often been put, whether I think going personally to the offices is a good plan. I should say *no*, if this visiting means running round to strange offices and taking up a man's time by suggestions which he would prefer to receive by post and could dismiss in two seconds; and this he can hardly do in courtesy to a woman visitor. Of course, if a woman is very prepossessing and charming, these visits might tell in her favour; but I should still prefer that she relied so far as possible on ordinary business-like methods. I think, however, that an *occasional* visit to an editor for whom one works is a distinctly wise step. He learns to remember the individuality of his contributor.

"There is not, I think, anything more for me to say, beyond a word about the desirability of this journalism. It has, of course, its less attractive side—what wage-earning for women involving the rough and tumble of the world has not? —and I think there are few women of a true type who do not feel that they have within them powers and influences which were destined for something less sordid than wage-earning. But there is no need to write what is base or vulgar, though much of our written word may be frivolous and futile; and if we will but look upon our journalism as a harmless means to an end, the end which saves us from being a burden upon others already over-weighted by the struggle for

existence, and make, not our bread - winning
drudgery, but our inner life the predominant one,
I think we can escape with not more soil and dust
upon our souls than are inevitable when we are
called upon to fight the world in order that we
may breathe and live in it."

PART VII.

THE OUTLOOK.

As I have said, feminine journalism and the typical feminine journalist respectively represent work and the exponent of this work, which no one with any sense of the dignity and responsibility of journalism can regard without regret and even a feeling of just anger at the deterioration, æsthetic and moral, that both exhibit at the present moment. Yet it would be equally foolish and profitless to invest this with any permanent element.

It is a singular fact that the two pioneer women journalists remain in their respective *genre* the most accomplished and perfect mistresses of the art that have been yielded by any country or generation. Madame de Guizot, one of the most thoughtful and far-seeing of women in an age when women justly claimed perfect intellectual equality with men of the keenest thought and reasoning power, stamped her newspaper writing with the penetration and force that are to be found in the best journalism of men writers. Madame de Girardin, as Gautier correctly

said, transformed the every day chronicling of the
hour into a new and exquisite art, as capable of
giving pleasure to a refined sense as any other
branch of letters.

To compare the witty, graceful, urbane pages
of Madame de Girardin, whether her theme be a
ball, or a hunt, or even the description of a
woman's gown, containing not a single per-
sonality or even name of any person prominent
in Society, with, for example, the "Ladies'
Page" in some of our most prominent Society
papers, from the pens of the most successful women
of the day, is to realise with consternation and
humiliation what we have lost. Style, charm,
and that light but not flippant handling
which embellishes the most commonplace
trifle, and that at one time was the
hall-mark of a cultivated woman of the great
world, have been replaced by an inconceivable
vulgarity and bad taste, in which the appearance
and marriage prospects of young girls hardly out
of the schoolroom are freely discussed. We have
reached a period of manners when the newspaper
publicity of a woman and her affairs is looked
upon as the measure of her success.

In one of the high class Society journals that I
picked up the other day I read: "It was a somewhat dull affair at Lady D.'s, or at least it would
have been if it had not been for pretty Lady Mar-
jorie —— who soon made things 'go the pace,' as

our sporting men folk say. Lady D.'s girl, who has grown up quite nice-looking, was far from becomingly dressed."

This specimen of good taste, it may safely be said, would have been regarded by the spiritual, witty Madame de Girardin as suited for the shop-keeping classes; and that mocking smile never far from her beautiful lips, according to Gautier, certainly would have appeared upon learning that it was put into the mouth of an aristocratic lady journalist who was discussing her hostess, Lady D.

Nine-tenths of the women's journalism of the day is in this strain, and its declension from its highest expression in France, and from the standard for many years sustained in this country by Harriet Martineau, Frances Power Cobbe, Mrs. Lynn Linton, and others, down to its present low —one hopes lowest—level, must always remain a puzzle in face of the diffusion of education amongst women. No doubt the explanation is partly to be found in the fact, that whereas fifty years ago the women journalists were picked members of their sex, possessing scholarship and culture, added to a high sense of responsibility, to-day every semi-educated girl attracted by an easy mode of earning a small income, takes to journalism, and with the present standard prevailing, as a rule possesses the requisite qualifications.

Yet no one who has any observation can doubt that women's journalism is capable of fulfilling a great modern mission—nothing less than that of giving the vast majority of middle-class women all the education they receive after leaving school, and of influencing them, whether consciously or not, in the direction of simplicity, good taste, good sense, moderation, and duty. It is impossible to overrate the force of this influence, or to measure the effect on national ideals if instead of the present gospel of extravagance, snobbery, the mad pursuit of dress, the craze for excitement, spending, and materialistic pleasures, there was substituted in the Woman's Press one of Simplicity, Light, and Sweetness; its apostles women of education and refinement and artistic tastes, and above all penetrated with the responsibility of their task.

PART VIII.

SOCIETIES, AGENCIES, AND BOOKS.

Societies and Clubs.

THE INCORPORATED SOCIETY OF AUTHORS, 39, Old Queen Street, Westminster, S.W.

Bonâ-fide journalists can join this Society for the annual subscription of one guinea (5 dolls.), and will find it very useful. The Society will advise on publishing without any further fee, examine agreements, and recover payments from publishers and editors. It has also a useful monthly organ called the *Author*, which is sent free to members, and contains much useful information.

THE WRITERS' CLUB, Hastings House, Norfolk Street, Strand, London, W.C.

This club, the subscription for which is £1 10s. 6d. (7½ dolls.) is composed of women writers and journalists. It has social afternoons, and is useful in bringing the young journalist into acquaintanceship with members of the craft. It also affords a convenient place for reading, writing, refreshment, &c.

INSTITUTE OF JOURNALISTS, Tudor Street, New
Bridge Street, London, E.C.

The Institute aims at the promotion of what-
ever may tend to the elevation of the status
and improvement of the qualification of journalists. Members can obtain advice with reference to the status of journals with which
they may wish to enter into engagements,
legal assistance in difficulties, &c. There is a
provident fund in connection with the Institute,
and also a charitable fund for the benefit of the
orphans of journalists. Members must have
had three years' practical experience of the
profession, and be still engaged in it. Women
are admitted on the same terms as men.

ROYAL LITERARY FUND, 6, Adelphi Terrace, London, W.C.

Assists necessitous authors, their widows
and orphans, or mothers and sisters.

NEWSPAPER PRESS FUND, 11, Garrick Street,
Covent Garden, London, W.C.

Assists necessitous journalists, their widows
and orphans.

SOCIETY OF WOMEN JOURNALISTS, Granville House,
3, Arundel Street, Strand, London, W.C.

An association composed exclusively of
women. The subscription is a guinea (5 dolls.),
and for this, in addition to other advantages,
legal advice is given.

Principal News Agencies.

CENTRAL NEWS, LTD., 5, New Bridge Street, Ludgate Circus, London, E.C.

Mainly news paragraphs, telegrams, &c.

NATIONAL PRESS AGENCY, LTD., Whitefriars House, 6, Carmelite Street, Fleet Street, London, E.C.

All kinds of Press matter, stories, London letters, news, &c.

PRESS ASSOCIATION, 14, New Bridge Street, London, E.C.

Similar to the National Press Agency.

BOLTON NEWSPAPER FICTION BUREAU. (Messrs. Tillotson and Son, Ltd., Bolton.)

Supplies to newspapers fiction by popular authors.

NORTHERN NEWSPAPER SYNDICATE, Head office, Kendal.

Suplies the London and Provincial Press with (signed) articles on a variety of subjects, serial fiction, and short stories.

Useful Books.

THE LITERARY YEAR BOOK (George Allen, 156, Charing Cross Road, W.C.).

Contains much useful information with regard to newspapers and magazines and publishers, the kind of contributions they accept, the rates they pay, &c.   Price 2s. 6d. (60c.) net.

WILLING'S PRESS GUIDE (Jas. Willing, jun., Ltd., 160, Piccadilly, W.). Price 1s. (24c.).

SELL'S PRESS DIRECTORY (Sell's Advertising Agency, 156 and 158, Fleet Street, E.C.). Price 7s. 6d. ($1.80).

THE WRITER'S YEAR BOOK (Writer's Year Book Co., Granville House, Arundel Street, Strand, London, W.C.). Price 1s. 6d. (36c.).

A directory for professional writers giving addresses of, and details as to conditions under which contributions are accepted by, the principal British newspapers, magazines, &c.; and other useful information.

PRACTICAL JOURNALISM: HOW TO ENTER THEREON AND SUCCEED. By John Dawson. New Edition, revised, with additional chapters (L. Upcott Gill, Bazaar Buildings, Drury Lane, London, W.C.). Price 1s. (24c.).

A capital handbook for all who think of writing for the Press.

INDEX.